Explode 4
The Code

Nancy Hall Rena Price

Educators Publishing Service

Cambridge and Toronto

Educators Publishing Service
800.225.5750
www.epsbooks.com

Text illustrations by Laura Price and Alan Price

Cover by Hugh Price

Copyright © 2001, 1999, 1998, 1994, 1990, 1989, 1984, 1977 by Educators Publishing Service. All rights reserved. No part of this book may be reproduced or utilized in any form or by any electronic or mechanical means, including photocopying, without permission in writing from the publisher.

Printed in the U.S.A.
ISBN 0-8388-1463-8

6 7 8 9 10 CUR 09 08 07 06 05

Lesson 1

RULE: Sometimes 2 little words are put together to make 1 word. The new word is called a compound word.

wind + mill = windmill

Draw a line between the 2 little words in each compound word below:

in|side	catfish
hillside	sunset
homesick	pancake
maybe	bedtime
upset	himself

RULE: 2 little words put together make a compound word.

wind + mill = windmill

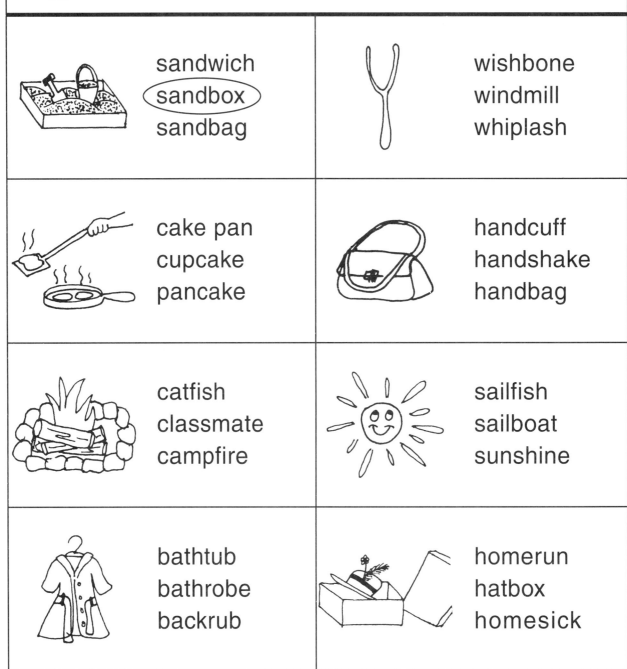

◯ the compound word that matches the picture:

sandwich
~~sandbox~~
sandbag

wishbone
windmill
whiplash

cake pan
cupcake
pancake

handcuff
handshake
handbag

catfish
classmate
campfire

sailfish
sailboat
sunshine

bathtub
bathrobe
backrub

homerun
hatbox
homesick

	Spell:		Write:
	mend (wind)	will (mill)	_windmill_
	pump drum	stuck stick	_____
	sun fun	set seat	_____
	cut cup	kick cake	_____
	pin flag	pole hole	_____
	dish dash	pan pin	_____
	bass base	hall ball	_____

Read, write, and "X" it:

pancake _pancake_			
pigpen _____			
bathtub _____			
anthill _____			
lampshade _____			
sandbox _____			
fishpond _____			

4

Yes or no?

	No	Yes
Can you catch a windmill?	☒	☐
Will a wishbone bring luck?	☐	☐
Can you sit on a flagpole?	☐	☐
Will a rosebud smell sweet?	☐	☐
Will a classmate sleep in a pigpen?	☐	☐
Are you upset if you are homesick?	☐	☐
Can you bake homemade cupcakes?	☐	☐

Pick a word to fit each sentence:

skyline	fishbone	~~baseball~~
fishpond	sunshine	flagpole
bedtime	bathtub	campfire

Let's play a game of _baseball_ .

It's fun to sit by the _____ .

You raise the flag on the _____ .

The _____ melts the snow.

Put the plug and the soap in the _____ .

At the end of the day it is _____ .

See if you can catch a fish in the _____ .

"X" it:

Dave is inside the pigpen.	☒	
Dave is inside the sandbox.	☐	
Hank is glad to sit on the cupcake.	☐	
Hank is safe inside his playpen.	☐	
The baseball bat will not fit in the lunchbox.	☐	
She digs in the sandbox with a drumstick.	☐	
Gus sails in the bathtub at sunset.	☐	
Gus drops his handbag in the fishpond.	☐	
The cupcakes on the sailboat are homemade.	☐	
The flat pancakes are in the hatbox.	☐	
The big wishbone is on the lampshade.	☐	
The fishbone is stuck in the windmill.	☐	
The tomcat hunts in the trashcans.	☐	
The tomcat jumps into the dishpan.	☐	

Write it:

	<u>sunshine</u> _____
	_____
	_____
	_____
	_____
	_____
	_____

Lesson 2

RULE: Sometimes an ending such as –ful, –ing, –est, –ed, or –ness is added to a word to make a new word.

jump + ing = jumping

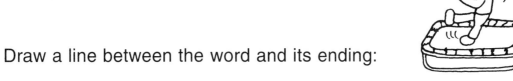

Draw a line between the word and its ending:

sad/ness	hope/ful
wish/ing	glad/ness
fresh/est	slant/ed
still/ness	help/ful
black/est	pinch/ing

RULE: Sometimes an ending such as –ful, –ing, –est, –ed, or –ness is added to a word to make a new word.

jump + ing = jumping

◯ the word that matches the picture.

trustful
tankful
thankful

longest
likeness
illness

thickness
sickest
skillful

fixing
fistful
fishing

stealing
spanking
splashing

wished
twisted
hinted

handing
hanging
banging

careful
clearing
cupful

	Spell:		Write:
	hang hand	ful ness	_____
	cap cup	ful less	_____
	sing swing	est ing	_____
	brush rush	ing ly	_____
	best wilt	less ed	_____
	sad safe	ful ness	_____
	rest rich	est ed	_____

Read, write, and "X" it:

rocking _____			
thankful _____			
singing _____			
gladness _____			
rusted _____			
brushing _____			
handful _____			

Yes or no?

	No	Yes
Can a plant become wilted?	☐	☐
Will you be careful when crossing a street?	☐	☐
Can a cupful of rocks be melted?	☐	☐
Can a drumstick go fishing in a stream?	☐	☐
Is brushing teeth helpful?	☐	☐
Is it restful to sit in a rocking chair?	☐	☐
Will a bathtub say it is thankful?	☐	☐

Pick a word to fit each sentence:

thankful	fishing	cupful
rusted	careful	stillness
rocking	sickness	longest

I felt _____ that I was safe.

The twins sat in the _____ chair.

Be _____ if you ride a bike in the street.

With bait and rod we will go _____ .

If a truck is old, it may be _____ .

Spot has long ears and the _____ tail.

You need a _____ of milk to make a cake.

"X" it:

The rusted train is standing on the track.	☐	
The rusted chain is inside the truck.	☐	
She is brushing her long hair.	☐	
She is rushing to the rocking chair.	☐	
Ray is painting the boards with a brush.	☐	
Ray is helping us pack the trunks.	☐	
We are thankful for the grandest meal.	☐	
We are thinking of singing in class.	☐	
The hopeful dog begs at the feet of his pal.	☐	
The helpful dog is bringing in the mail.	☐	
Jane is drinking a thick eggnog.	☐	
Jane is standing on an anthill.	☐	
Nick is showing that his bike is the fastest.	☐	
Nick is careful not to skate on the deepest pond.	☐	

Write it:

	_____ ness
	_____ ing
	_____ est
	_____ ing
	_____ ing
	_____ ful
	_____ ing

Lesson 3

RULE: When 2 consonants stand between 2 vowels, the word is usually divided between the consonants – vc/cv

rab / bit

Draw a line between the consonants:

lesson	attic
happen	gallon
summer	gossip
bottom	pepper
ballot	common

RULE: When 2 consonants stand between 2 vowels, the word is usually divided between the consonants – vc/cv

rab · bit

⬭ the word that matches the picture:

thin · nest
ten · nis
traf · fic

slip · per
sup · per
sip · ping

rob · ber
rub · ber
rib · bon

dim · mer
blos · som
but · ton

muf · fin
mit · ten
mop · ping

zig · zag
zip · per
kit · ten

tun · nel
trap · per
traf · fic

bon · net
bot · tom
din · ner

	Spell:		Write:
	sup sap	ger per	_____
	tan tun	net nel	_____
	met mit	ten net	_____
	ham hem	mer met	_____
	lat let	ted ter	_____
	lit kit	net ten	_____
	track traf	fic cif	_____

Read, write, and "X" it:

butter _____			
rabbit _____			
muffin _____			
ladder _____			
mitten _____			
ribbon _____			
hammer _____			

Yes or no?

	No	Yes
Can a helpful kitten try to do a lesson?	☐	☐
Will dinner be the biggest meal of the day?	☐	☐
Can a muffin have butter and jam on top?	☐	☐
Can a letter be put in a mailbox?	☐	☐
Is it madness to sleep in a tunnel?	☐	☐
Can a hammer and nails be useful?	☐	☐
Can the longest ladder go fishing?	☐	☐

Pick a word to fit each sentence:

traffic	tennis	happen
rabbits	ladder	pepper
button	summer	attic

Is it fun to play _____ ?

You keep big trunks in the _____ .

To reach the top shelf you need a _____ .

He has three soft pet _____ .

I lost a _____ from my coat.

The cab will honk in the _____ .

You may use _____ on your eggs.

"X" it:

He is at the bottom of the flagpole.	☐	
He is standing on the biggest bathmat.	☐	
The kitten is sitting in the hottest bathtub.	☐	
The kitten is slipping into the pond.	☐	
He had muffins and butter for lunch.	☐	
He had mittens and slippers in his lunchbox.	☐	
She plays tennis on the ladder.	☐	
She puts the ribbon on the letter.	☐	
The robber is stealing the rabbit.	☐	
The rabbit puts handcuffs on the robber.	☐	
The kittens stop the traffic.	☐	
The muffins play hide-and-seek.	☐	
The crash happens in the tunnel.	☐	
A gallon of milk drips in the tunnel.	☐	

Write it:

	_____
	_____
	_____
	_____
	_____
	_____
	_____

Lesson 4

RULE: When a word has 2 consonants that come between 2 vowels, the word is divided into syllables between the 2 consonants – vc/cv

nap / kin

Draw a line between the syllables in each word below:

under	number
tablet	kidnap
problem	velvet
absent	thunder
expense	public

RULE: When a word has 2 consonants that come between 2 vowels, the word is divided into syllables between the 2 consonants – vc/cv

nap / kin

 the word that matches the picture:

con • tent
con • test
cos • tume

un • less
un • der
sum • mer

tem • per
tin • sel
thin • ner

won • der
win • ner
win • ter

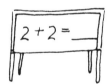

pub • lic
plas • tic
prob • lem

ad • mit
in • dex
es • cape

trip • lets
tin • gle
trum • pet

sel • dom
ex • pense
san • dal

	Spell:		Write:
	sag sig	lan nal	_____
	bis bas	kin ket	_____
	trum runt	pet pan	_____
	den dan	tist sit	_____
	mat mag	ten net	_____
	pan pin	tin cake	_____
	ban bat	dit din	_____

Read, write, and "X" it:

sandal _____			
padlock _____			
sister _____			
napkin _____			
costume _____			
contest _____			
picnic _____			

Yes or no?

	No	Yes
Will a napkin be made of velvet?	☐	☐
Is your sister a triplet?	☐	☐
Do you take a basket of food on a picnic?	☐	☐
Can a bandit escape after you catch him?	☐	☐
Can a brass trumpet whisper?	☐	☐
Is it safe to play in traffic?	☐	☐
Will a dentist fix your finger?	☐	☐

Pick a word to fit each sentence:

triplets	winter	tinsel
admit	under	absent
umpire	unpack	public

Three kids that are the same can be _____ .

When it sleets and snows it is _____ .

You can trim the tree with balls and _____ .

We can sit _____ the shade tree when it is hot.

The _____ calls the plays in a a baseball game.

If you are not in class, you are _____ .

If you take things from a picnic basket, you _____ the lunch.

"X" it:

The bandit signals to his pal.	☐	
The band sings and plays.	☐	
The problem has a big mistake.	☐	
The master has a pet goblin.	☐	
The dentist has plastic teeth.	☐	
The dentist has big sandals.	☐	
The triplets are sitting in a nutshell.	☐	
The picnic basket is full of tinsel.	☐	
The umpire signals with a napkin.	☐	
The umpire shakes his finger.	☐	
I put on a witch costume.	☐	
Allen wins a ribbon at the contest.	☐	
The thunder stops the picnic.	☐	
My sister is playing the trumpet.	☐	

Write it:

	_____
	_____
	_____
	_____
	_____
	_____
	_____

*For further reinforcement see Book 4½, pp.1–9.

Words can be divided into syllables:
1. between 2 little words — **wind/mill**
2. between a word and its ending—**jump/ing**
3. between 2 consonants that are the same—**rab/bit**
4. between 2 consonants that come between 2 vowels—vc/cv—**nap/kin**

Draw a line between the syllables in each word below:

collect	invite
plastic	splendid
hopeful	hello
admit	backpack
gossip	index

To help read these words, think of the rules to divide words into syllables.

 the word to match the picture:

invite
unlock
unsafe

public
puppet
pumpkin

slapstick
stamped
slanted

swinging
slippers
slingshot

chipmunk
chopstick
chicken

whipping
whisper
whisker

master
monster
mitten

member
number
madman

	Spell:		Write:
	san sun	shin shine	_____
	kiss sick	ing ang	_____
	lip lap	stack stick	_____
	mit met	ten net	_____
	swing sing	ing ong	_____
	wish whis	kers ken	_____
	slip ship	pen per	_____

Read, write, and "X" it:

puppet _____			
hammock _____			
slingshot _____			
handshake _____			
chipmunk _____			
hanging _____			
slanted _____			

Yes or no?

	No	Yes
Can he play with puppets by himself?	☐	☐
Can you play the trumpet with lipstick on?	☐	☐
Will a chipmunk shave his whiskers?	☐	☐
Can you make a slingshot with a rubber band?	☐	☐
Will a gumdrop be made of plastic?	☐	☐
Is it a mistake to kiss a monster?	☐	☐
Do hands go inside slippers and feet in mittens?	☐	☐

"X" it:

Chip is running on a splendid day.	☐	
Chip is swinging on a sling shot.	☐	
The monster rests in the hammock.	☐	
The monster is rushing to the hilltop.	☐	
A man with whiskers collects trash.	☐	
The firetruck whips into the driveway.	☐	
Joan unlocks the biggest chest.	☐	
Joan unpacks the cheese and crackers.	☐	
The chipmunks are wishing for summer.	☐	
The chipmunks are sipping the eggnog.	☐	
The puppets are swinging by strings.	☐	
The pup has a leash made of the thinnest string.	☐	
We are swimming in rubber tires.	☐	
The slippers are hanging beside the fire.	☐	

Write it:

☀	_____
👫	_____
👞	_____
👹	_____
🏠	_____
🧤	_____
👧	_____

39

Open and Closed Syllables

Dō – rā – mē

Open Syllables: When a syllable ends with a vowel, it is an open syllable. The vowel is long and says its name as in **mē.**

Hŭm – hǐm – hŏm – hŭm

Closed Syllables: When a syllable ends with a consonant, it is a closed syllable. The vowel is short as in **mĕn.**

Make the mouth show the syllable open or closed

1. met

2. he

3. go

4. Jo

5. hi

6. yet

7. bag

8. mob

9. we

10. be

11. ho

12. jog

13. dot

14. kid

15. fin

16. me

17. so

18. fat

Mark the vowels in these syllables long (–) as in mē, or short (◡) as in měn.

1. ŏb

2. spo

3. ki

4. brid

5. de

6. cha

7. ep

8. twe

9. ag

10. shug

11. fu

12. bist

13. ye

14. tho

15. bim

16. fant

RULE: When 1 consonant stands between 2 vowels, the word is usually divided after the first vowel—v/cv. The first syllable is *open*, and the vowel will say its name.

rō / bŏt

Draw a line between the syllables so the first vowel will say its name.

silent	omit
minus	basic
stupid	demand
bonus	crocus
total	relax

RULE: If a word is divided after the first vowel, the first syllable will be open and the vowel will say its name.

<h2 style="text-align:center">rō / bŏt</h2>

 the word that matches the picture:

	pep • per pa • per pi • per		ze • bra zip • per ze • ro
	bit • ter bi • ting bit • ing		sil • ent si • lent si • lo
	ba • con beck • on bac • on		ti • mer tig • er ti • ger
	hum • id hum • an hu • man		pil • ot pi • lot pil • low

	Spell:		Write:
	ti tig	re ger	_____
	ba back	one con	_____
	bro brok	ken een	_____
	pil pi	lot ote	_____
	mus mu	ice sic	_____
	tu tul	ide lip	_____
	stu stud	dent ent	_____

Read, write, and "X" it:

diver			
_____			
motel			
_____			
frozen			
_____			
erase			
_____			
polite			
_____			
skating			
_____			
robot			
_____			

Yes or no?

	No	Yes
Can a robot eat a tulip?	☐	☐
Will a student use paper to make an airplane?	☐	☐
Is a clover as big as a tiger?	☐	☐
Can you read the paper in a hotel?	☐	☐
Can you bake a cake in the shape of a pilot?	☐	☐
Will a motel go skating with a seagull?	☐	☐
Can a human relax in a hammock?	☐	☐

Pick a word to fit each sentence:

paper	human	hoping
frozen	silent	erase
tiger	motel	driving

In winter the lake is _____ .

A _____ has a long tail and can bite.

I can stay and sleep in a _____ .

Each of us is a _____ being.

My sister is _____ the truck.

If students are reading, it is best to be _____ .

The pilot is flying _____ to win a prize for safe flying.

"X" it:

The student is hoping to get a prize. ☐ The student is hopping on a paper rug. ☐	
Steve gets a zero on his math paper. ☐ Steve is biting the snowman. ☐	
A pilot can be a hero. ☐ A pilot is hiding in the tree. ☐	
A rabbit is staying at the hotel. ☐ A robot is stamping on the hotel. ☐	
Fran is skating with the tiger. ☐ Fran is baking with the tiger. ☐	
Chuck has taken a bunch of tulips to the sink. ☐ Chuck has broken the side of the vase. ☐	
Ellen is sitting in the nutshell. ☐ Ellen is riding on the music note. ☐	

Write it:

	_____
	_____
	_____
	_____
	_____
	_____
	_____

*For further reinforcement see Book 4½, pp. 10–18.

Lesson 8

RULE: When a word has 1 consonant between 2 vowels, sometimes the word is divided *after* the consonant — vc/v. The first syllable is now *closed*, and the vowel sound is short.

sĕv / ĕn 7

Draw a line between the syllables so the first vowel is short:

solid	panic
rapid	British
tonic	chapel
lemon	level
finish	comet

RULE: When a word has 1 consonant between 2 vowels, sometimes the word is divided after the consonant — vc/v. The first syllable is now closed.

sĕv / ĕn

◯ the word to match the picture:

	sev • er sev • en se • ven		po • lar po • lish pol • ish
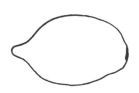	le • mon lim • it lem • on		show • boat sho • vel shov • el
	so • lid sal • ad sa • lad		cam • el can • non ca • mel
	ro • bin ro • bot rob • in		deb • it ped • al pe • dal

	Spell:		Write:
	fi fin	nist ish	_____
	rob ro	bent in	_____
	dra drag	on gone	_____
	pla plan	eet et	_____
	cam ca	melt el	_____
	cab ca	in ine	_____
	wa wag	on gone	_____

53

Read, write, and "X" it:

comics _____			
closet _____			
medal _____			
shovel _____			
vanish _____			
travel _____			
seven _____			

54

Yes or no?

	No	Yes
Will a lemon visit a wagon?	☐	☐
Do log cabins have windows?	☐	☐
Do planets travel in the sky?	☐	☐
Is a robin as big as a camel?	☐	☐
Will you polish a bike to keep it clean?	☐	☐
Will you see dragons in prison?	☐	☐
Do you like to finish the salad in the bowl?	☐	☐

Pick a word to fit each sentence:

salad	comics	travel
lemon	prison	robin
polish	closet	finish

A robber may be sent to _____ .

You mix greens in a bowl to make _____ .

The _____ laid seven eggs in a nest.

We keep coats and hats in the _____ .

When you go on a trip, you _____ .

To _____ means "to rub with a cloth."

A lime is green; a _____ is yellow.

"X" it:

The dragon is sitting on the planet.	☐	
The dragon is hiding in the lunchbox.	☐	
A camel is inside the closet.	☐	
A camel is standing beside the cabin.	☐	
Rob made a model of the wagon.	☐	
Rob ate his meal in the wagon.	☐	
Seven ants got lost in the prison.	☐	
The biggest ant is hanging from the pedal.	☐	
Jean can polish the silver medal.	☐	
Jean shovels snow on the planet.	☐	
My kitten can pedal the bike fast.	☐	
The tiger cannot catch the cat.	☐	
The robin is filling the gas tank.	☐	
The robin travels to the treetop.	☐	

Write it:

7	_____
	_____
	_____
	_____
	_____
	_____
	_____

*For further reinforcement see Book 4½, pp. 19–27.

Lesson 9

RULE: When a 2 syllable word ends in y, the y says /ē/. The y takes the consonant before it to make the last syllable.

sun / ny

Draw a line between the syllables:

si|ly	lazy
baby	funny
happy	dolly
crazy	bandy
dizzy	ivy

59

RULE: When a 2 syllable word ends in y, the y says /ē/, and takes the consonant before it to make the last syllable.

sun • ny

 the word that matches the picture:

---

jol • ly
jel • lo
jel • ly

can • ned
can • dy
camp • ing

---

tin • ny
ti • ny
tim • id

ug • ly
gol • ly
lug • ging

chil • dren
rich • est
chil • ly

fit • ting
fif • ty
lof • ty

sil • ky
skin • ny
stin • ky

can • dy
can • ning
cam • py

	Spell:		Write:
20 ☆	twin (twen) (ty) ly		twenty
	(bun) dim ly (ny)		bunny
	(po) bo my ny		pony
	no (hap) (py) ble		happy
	ba da (by) thing		baby
	stin (skin) ky) (ny)		skiny
	dot (pup) (py) ty		puppy

61

Read, write, and "X" it:

navy			
navy			
grassy			
grassy			
clumsy			
clumsy			
windy			
windy			
baby			
baby			
ivy			
ivy			
fifty			
fifty			

Yes or no?

	No	Yes
Can a tiny baby sleep in a playpen?	☐	☐
Will you see a pony rowing a boat?	☐	☐
Can Tommy sit on a grassy hill?	☐	☐
Is a kitty as big as a ship in the navy?	☐	☐
Can a bag of candy run quickly?	☐	☐
Will you be happy to play with a puppy?	☐	☐
Is it silly to eat fifty pancakes?	☐	☐

Pick a word to fit each sentence:

windy	twenty	bunny
candy	swiftly	clumsy
happy	baby	ivy

When you get a gift, you feel _____ .

Trees bend and blow on a _____ day.

The Easter _____ hides eggs and candy in a basket.

When I am late, I run _____ to catch the train.

The number after nineteen is _____ .

My dentist tells me to eat just a tiny bit of _____ .

_____ is a vine with glossy leaves.

"X" it:

The chubby bunny is eating in the closet.	☐	
The chubby bunny is sitting on the gate.	☐	
Becky is letting the pony munch the carrot.	☐	
Becky puts the carrot on the stony path.	☐	
Katy has bitten into the big cupcake.	☐	
Katy was bitten by a tiny dragon in the sandbox.	☐	
The puppy is napping after swimming in the lake.	☐	
The puppy is happy swimming in the lake.	☐	
Polly is playing with the tiny kitty.	☐	
Polly is playing tennis in a tiny dress.	☐	
Jimmy has a crazy time with the gravy.	☐	
Jimmy has a lazy time in the navy.	☐	
The kitty is running to hide under the buggy.	☐	
The kitty is happy to be driving in the hot rod.	☐	

Write it:

50	_____
	_____
	_____
	_____
20	_____
	_____
	_____

66   *For further reinforcement see Book 4½, pp. 73–81.

Lesson 10

RULE: When –le is at the end of a word, it takes the consonant before to make the last syllable.

ap / ple

Draw a line between the syllables:

thim|ble	sam|ple
snug|gle	stab|le
jun|gle	sim|ple
brid|le	bat|tle
crad|le	pad|dle

RULE: When -le is at the end of a word, it takes the consonant before it to make the last syllable.

ap · ple

 the word that matches the picture:

rat · tle
~~pad · dle~~
pud · dle

tin · gle
thim · ble
twin · kle

ham · mer
han · dle
hang · ing

jig · gle
jug · gle
jun · gle

scrab · ble
crac · kle
cra · dle

sad · dle
man · tle
sad · der

cat · tle
ket · tle
kit · ten

stum · ble
snug · gle
stam · mer

	Spell:		Write:
	la ta	dle ble	_____
	bit lit	tle gle	_____
	can con	ble dle	_____
	sad sta	dle kle	_____
	dot bot	ter tle	_____
	cra bro	dle ble	_____
	nib mid	dle kle	_____

Read, write, and "X" it:

bugle			
handle			
puzzle			
bubble			
maple			
juggle			
paddle			

70

Yes or no?

	No	Yes
Can you paddle a boat inside a bottle?	☐	☐
Is it fun to blow soap bubbles?	☐	☐
Do you put a kettle on the stove?	☐	☐
Will cattle sleep in a cradle?	☐	☐
Will a needle vanish in the grass?	☐	☐
Can a puzzle fit on the table?	☐	☐
Is a rock a little pebble?	☐	☐

Pick a word to fit each sentence:

saddle	bottle	table
apple	paddle	cradle
bugle	stumble	puzzle

We keep milk in a _____ .

You sit at the _____ when you eat.

If you trip on a rug, you _____ .

The baby sleeps in a _____ .

With a _____ you can play music.

Use the _____ to steer the boat.

You sit in a _____ to ride a pony.

"X" it:

The bunny can paddle the boat.	☐	
The bunny can saddle the pony.	☐	
Jeff is clumsy with the candle.	☐	
Jeff is careful with the candy.	☐	
Twenty apples are on the tree.	☐	
The ugly apples are taking a trip.	☐	
Allen is playing the bugle in the navy.	☐	
Allen paddles a boat in the gravy.	☐	
The pony has a saddle on his back.	☐	
The pony is standing in a puddle.	☐	
A puppy and a kitty had a battle.	☐	
A puppy topples the table on the kitten.	☐	
The baby is sleeping in a cozy cradle.	☐	
The funny baby drinks his bottle in his playpen.	☐	

Write it:

	_____
	_____
	_____
	_____
	_____
	_____
	_____

74

*For further reinforcement see Book 4½, pp. 82–90.

Lesson 11

RULE: Sometimes 2 vowels together in a syllable make 1 sound. This is a vowel digraph syllable: *ai, ay, ee, ea, oa, ow*. The sound is the long sound of the first vowel. The syllable *may* or *may not* have a consonant with it.

fif<u>teen</u> 15   **<u>ea</u>gle**

⬭ the vowel digraph syllables in the words below.

be(tween)	needle
oatmeal	below
meanest	faithful
sweetness	raisin
relay	teapot

Look for the vowel digraph syllables: 2 vowels making 1 sound.

cr<u>ay</u> on

◯ the word to match the picture below:

rab • bit
ro • bot
row • boat

fel • low
fol • low
fold • ed

de • cay
diz • zy
dai • sy

hate • ful
hay • stack
drum • stick

bee • tle
bat • tle
bot • tle

ant • hill
ear • ring
air • plane

paint • brush
hair • brush
hop • scotch

stair • way
snow • man
scare • crow

	Spell:		Write:
	seal sail	bone boat	_____
	rail rain	bow bowl	_____
	fif ful	teen ten	_____
	ea ai	dle gle	_____
	plow play	pan pen	_____
	toast blow	er est	_____
	ween win	blow dow	_____

Read, write, and "X" it:

sweeper _____			
peacock _____			
teacher _____			
needle _____			
railroad _____			
bowling _____			
tepee _____			

Yes or no?

	No	Yes
Can a teacher have fifteen students?	☐	☐
Will a snowman follow his shadow?	☐	☐
Do you eat oatmeal when you are bowling?	☐	☐
Can an eagle paint with its elbow?	☐	☐
Can you put butter on raisin toast?	☐	☐
Will a scarecrow need a raincoat?	☐	☐
Is it greedy to take all the roasted peanuts?	☐	☐

Pick a word to fit each sentence:

snowman	toaster	rainbow
teacher	pillow	yellow
mailbox	reading	painter

The _____ explains the lesson to the class.

The _____ needs a ladder and a paintbrush.

We make toast in the _____ .

A bed has a blanket and a _____ .

I went to my _____ to get my letters.

On a snowy day we will make a big _____ .

After it rains, we may see a _____ .

"X" it:

My sister is mixing catsup and oatmeal in a bowl.	☐	
My uncle likes to bake meatloaf in a cake pan.	☐	
The window has a beetle painted on it.	☐	
The beetle is painting the window.	☐	
The snowy tugboat gets a bath.	☐	
The snowman is getting into the bathtub.	☐	
Dicky paints an eagle on his mailbox.	☐	
The eagle soars over the rainbow.	☐	
The scarecrow is going rowing.	☐	
The crow is skating on the tugboat.	☐	
The teapot is steaming on top of the tepee.	☐	
Sally has a teapot in the rowboat.	☐	
The trees make shadows on the window.	☐	
The weeping lady has her elbow stuck in the window.	☐	

Write it:

	_____
	_____
	_____
	_____
	_____
	_____
	_____

*For further reinforcement see Book 4½, pp. 46–54.

Lesson 12

Using the rules you have learned, draw a line between the syllables in each word below.

win|ter|time	remember
elastic	suddenly
invented	equipment
animal	calculate
happening	lemonade

You can use the rules you have learned to divide these words into syllables. Then you will be able to read them.

a word to match each picture:

	cattleman rattlesnake battleship	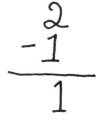	submitting sunbathing subtracting
	remember September distemper		unhappy unravel happiness
	chapstick chickadee chimpanzee		tomato potato rotate
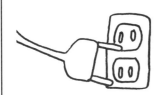	elastic eleven electric		October acrobat octopus

	Spell:			Write:
	val al	me en	tine nit	_____
	dum bum	led ble	bay bee	_____
	at to	ma mi	to ty	_____
	en am	vel to	ope op	_____
	go grass	hat hop	py per	_____
	oc ic	to at	pu pus	_____
	but bat	ter ten	fly try	_____

85

Read, write, and "X" it:

volcano _____			
hospital _____			
crocodile _____			
telescope _____			
cucumber _____			
eleven _____			
basketball _____			

Yes or no?

	No	Yes
Can a telescope help you see the sky?	☐	☐
Did you send the octopus a valentine?	☐	☐
Will a tomato go to the hospital?	☐	☐
Can a rattlesnake hide in the grass?	☐	☐
Is a grasshopper able to jump well?	☐	☐
Can a crocodile drive a cab?	☐	☐
Will a volcano sit at the table?	☐	☐

Pick a word to fit each sentence:

grasshopper	hospital	seventeen
butterfly	basketball	telescope
jellyfish	cucumbers	electric

Kids on a team can play _____ .

You may stay in a _____ if you are ill.

A lamp has a bulb, an _____ cord, and a plug.

I plant and grow _____ to put in salads.

We can see the planets with a _____ .

A _____ is a green insect that jumps in the grass.

A _____ has big wings and can fly.

"X" it:

The animal is chatting with a pal.	☐	
The chimpanzee has a telescope.	☐	
A rattlesnake is eating the electric lamp.	☐	
The rattlesnake is hidden in the envelope.	☐	
A butterfly is standing on top of the tomato.	☐	
Tommy is sitting on the butter dish.	☐	
The octopus sends a funny valentine.	☐	
The octopus bends seventeen legs.	☐	
The acrobat is swinging from the volcano.	☐	
The acrobat cannot see the volcano from his window.	☐	
That crocodile has a bumpy nose and no teeth.	☐	
That crocodile is drinking a big cup of tea.	☐	
The basketball team is standing on the bus.	☐	
The basketball team lands in the runway.	☐	

Write it:

	_____
	_____
17	_____
	_____
HAPPY BIRTH- DAY	_____
	_____
	_____

*For further reinforcement see Book 4½, pp. 91–99.

Book 4 — Posttest

Using the rules you have learned in this book, put a / between the syllables in the words below and mark the vowel in the first syllable long or short.

bā/con	cabin	silent	expense
refuse	later	demand	hungry
robin	rabbit	chosen	maple
finish	solid	wiggle	event
campus	velvet	stable	funny

Put a / between the syllables in the words below and mark the vowel in the first syllable long or short.

bŭn/dle	protect	faithful	habit
copper	tablet	absent	final
noble	bonus	simple	human
proper	radish	remain	elect
admit	program	nutmeg	jolly

Book 4 — Posttest

(Teacher dictated. See Key for Books 1 to 5.)

1.	thicket thimble tumble thinkable thinking	2.	resume reason reluct reseal result
3.	collate collar coffee collect colony	4.	shelter settle shelving shellfish shellac
5.	pertain pretest pretend pretense prevent	6.	blotchy bosom bolster bloated blossom
7.	explain explore expose explode expone	8.	demean benefit demolish bemoan beneath
9.	radiant rabbity raggedly radically rapidly	10.	prisoner persistent personnel president presiding

Book 4 — Posttest

(Teacher dictated. See Key for Books 1 to 5.)

1. _____

   _____

2. _____

   _____

3. _____

   _____

4. _____

   _____

5. _____

   _____

Book 4 — Posttest

Use the words to complete the sentences.

lazy	teacher	rabbit	papers
windows	begins	remain	candle

1. When the bell rings, the class _____ . The
_____ explains the daily lesson to the eager
students. They are never _____, but a tiny
fellow in the back row is playful. After class, three helpful
students _____ to shut the _____ ,
feed the _____, and grade the math
_____ .

splashing	bundle	mailbox	chilly
vanish	lucky	mittens	hoping

2. It is a _____ , wet, slippery day. I am rushing to
the _____ with lots of things to mail when I slip
and drop a _____ of letters in the street. Pulling
off my _____ , I begin picking up the
envelopes. A truck speeds by, _____ me and
crushing several letters under its tires. This is not my
_____ day!

basket	lemonade	baseball	chicken
human	tomato	dentist	shopping

3. After the _____ game, my teammates and I go
_____ at the store for a picnic supper. We fill
the _____ with things for a salad: cucumbers,
radishes, and a big red _____ . We add
_____ so we will have drumsticks at the picnic.
We plan to use frozen _____ to make a drink.